Stencils and Prints

Deri Robins

MINNETONKA, MINNESOTA

This edition published in 2006 in North America by
Two-Can Publishing
11571 K-Tel Drive
Minnetonka, MN 55343
www.two-canpublishing.com

Two-Can wishes to thank artist Shannon Steven for
her help with the American terms in this book.

Library of Congress CIP data on file

ISBN 1-58728-544-4

Written by Deri Robins
Designed by Wladek Szechter/Louise Morley
Edited by Sian Morgan/Matthew Harvey
Artwork by Melanie Grimshaw
Photographer Michael Wicks
With thanks to Victoria

Creative Director: Louise Morley
Editorial Manager: Jean Coppendale

Printed and bound in China

1 2 3 4 5 10 09 08 07 06

The words in **bold** are explained in the glossary on page 30.

Contents

Print kit

Most of the materials you'll need for your print kit are simple and cheap. Except for paints and brushes, you'll find everything you need around the house.

Paper and cardboard

You will need lots of newspaper to protect your work surface. You will also need paper to print on—anything from smooth sketch paper to **construction paper**. Scrap paper is always useful for trying out your ideas.

Papers with different textures

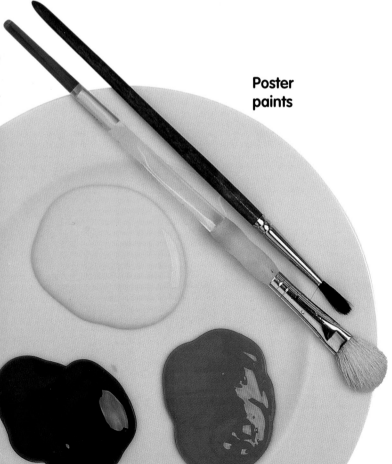

Poster paints

Cardboard is useful, so hold on to tubes and other packaging. Craft stores sell rigid paper for stenciling, but thin cardboard, like that used in cereal boxes, will work just as well.

Paints and inks

Poster paints are good for most printing jobs. Adding a little white glue or dishwashing detergent may keep the paint from drying out too fast. Printing inks are excellent, too.

For marbling, you will need oil paints. Remember that you need to thin oil paint with **mineral spirits** or turpentine, not water. Ask an adult to help you with these chemicals.

You'll need to buy special paints from a craft store for printing on fabric.

Ink

Stippling brush

Watercolor paints

Sponge roller

Tools and brushes

A **paint roller** is useful, but you can also get good results by applying the paint to your **printers** with a brush. For stenciling, you'll need a stippling brush with short, stubby bristles. An old toothbrush will be useful for **spattering**.

For some projects, you will need a **craft knife**. Handle it with care. Make sure that your work surface is protected and that an adult is present to help you.

Bits and pieces

One of the most useful parts of your print kit will be your junk box. Almost anything can be used for printing! Keep scraps of bubble wrap, fabric, cardboard, popsicle sticks, buttons, sponge, string, broken toys, and old tools. You'll find more suggestions throughout the book.

TIP

Keep scraps of fabric, colored paper, and candy wrappers, and paste them into a scrapbook or **sketchbook**. See how many shades of one color you can find.

Print effects

Any pattern made by pressing something down on a surface is printing. You've probably done it by accident! You can make beautiful shapes and **textures** from ordinary things, and make repeat patterns quickly. Let your imagination run wild!

Basic printing

You have pre-made printing tools at the ends of your arms! Dip your fingers, thumbs, and the sides of your hands into thick paint and press them down onto paper.

Found printers

There are plenty of found objects that make wonderful patterns, such as doilies, lace, the ends of straws, tools, keys, and fruit and vegetables.

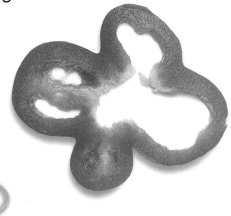

That's not all—try using your feet! Or put a thick layer of lipstick on your lips and press firmly on a piece of paper for luscious lip prints.

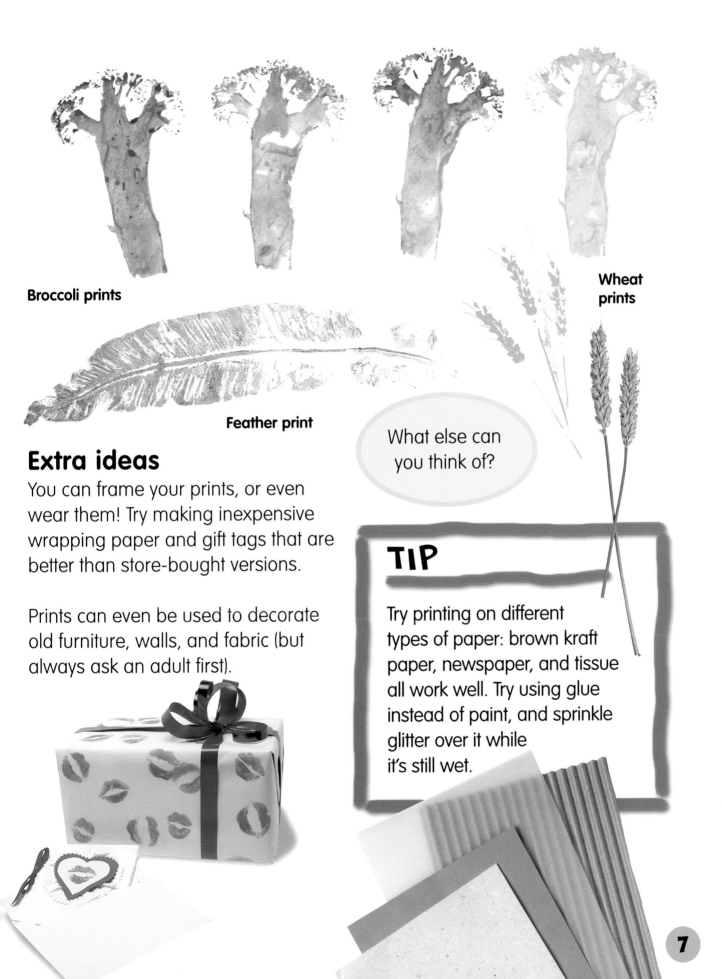

Broccoli prints

Wheat prints

Feather print

What else can you think of?

Extra ideas

You can frame your prints, or even wear them! Try making inexpensive wrapping paper and gift tags that are better than store-bought versions.

Prints can even be used to decorate old furniture, walls, and fabric (but always ask an adult first).

TIP

Try printing on different types of paper: brown kraft paper, newspaper, and tissue all work well. Try using glue instead of paint, and sprinkle glitter over it while it's still wet.

Mirror printing

This is one of the simplest and quickest ways to print.
The method is always the same, but every print is different.

Easy butterfly print

WHAT YOU NEED:
- Poster paints
- Paper
- A brush

1 Fold the paper in half. Open it up and paint some thick blobs on one side, roughly in the shape of half a butterfly. Make sure the paint goes right up to the fold, but not over it.

TIP

This works well for **symmetrical** shapes, such as flowers or leaves. See how many you can come up with.

1

2

2 Fold the paper over. Press down firmly, and then open it up.

TIP
Experiment with string of different weights and textures.

2 Fold a piece of paper in half, then open it up again, as you did for the butterfly print. Lay the strings randomly on one half of the paper, with the one end of each string hanging off the edge.

3 Close the paper over the string again. Press your hand firmly on the folded paper, as shown in the photo below. Pull the strings out from between the layers of paper. Unfold the paper and check out your swirly string picture!

String prints
String prints make fascinating, swirly patterns.

WHAT YOU NEED:
- String and scissors
- 3 small paint dishes
- Poster paints
- Paper

1 Cut three lengths of string. Put three different colors of poster paints into separate dishes. Put a piece of string in each dish. Turn them until they are well coated with paint.

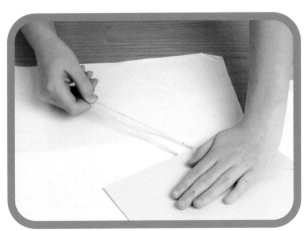

Block printing

One of the most common methods of printing is to use blocks. Block designs can be simple or complicated. You can make them yourself out of many different materials. The easiest are shapes cut out of cardboard.

Be a trash collector

Save as many different types of cardboard as possible. The kind with ridges is great for stripy prints. You can use the smooth side of the cardboard for printing blocks of color, and the edges for lines and curves. Use the ends of straws or cardboard tubes to make circles or ovals.

TIP

To make your blocks easier to use, glue a piece of cork or a large bead to the back to serve as a handle.

Print a greeting card

Try using blocks to make a simple greeting card. Make just one special card, or a whole batch that match.

WHAT YOU NEED:
- Poster paints • A brush
- Cardboard and paper

1 Sketch out your ideas for the card design on scrap paper. Keep the shapes simple.

2 Now cut out the shapes you need for your design. Use a separate printer for each color and shape.

3 Brush the largest printing block with paint. Then press it firmly onto the paper and peel it off to reveal the print beneath.

4 When the first color is dry, do the same with the smaller blocks until your picture is finished. Try not to smudge it!

5 Remember—anything can be a printer, even the end of a pen.

TIP

When you design your block printer, keep in mind that the print it makes will be a mirror image of the block!

More blocks!

You can never run out of ideas for block printers. Just look around your house! Glue objects to small pieces of wood for printers that you can use again and again.

Junk rules!

Cut shapes from foam, rubber, or sponges. Try printing with old keys, paper clips, dried pasta, buttons, buckles, old toys, or broken jewelry. Glue string to small pieces of wood or heavyweight cardboard in interesting shapes for simple prints. Almost anything will work!

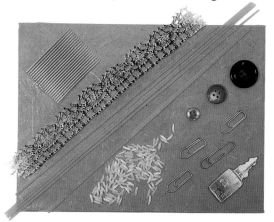

Let your imagination run wild—but don't forget to ask permission first!

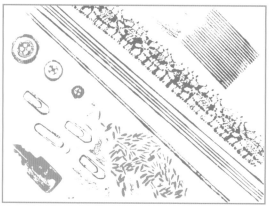

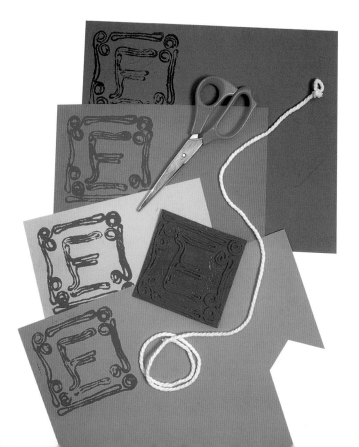

Make a bookplate

Glue string onto a block of wood in the shape of your initial. Remember to do it in reversed mirror writing. Add a few decorations, and use it to print your initial in the front of your books. (Let the paint dry completely before you close the covers!)

Sponge stamps

Sponge printers make crisp, clean prints. They are expensive to buy, but it's easy to make your own.

1 Draw a simple design on the soft side of the sponge.

2 Using a craft knife, carefully cut away the parts around the design.

3 Brush or roll paint over the raised surface. Then press the sponge onto the paper.

Sponges are also great for smaller patterns, such as wallpaper for a dolls' house. You can even print your own "postage stamps": ask an adult to use a sewing machine with no thread to "sew" the lines of holes.

Try printing a trail of animal tracks. Glue thin cutouts of footprints around the outside of a cardboard tube, and roll it across a piece of paper.

Prints from nature

Some of the most delicate prints are made from objects found in nature. Feathers, leaves, flowers, and wood all make lovely prints. With a few of these printers, you can make a pattern that would take hours to paint with a brush.

TIP

Leaves don't last very long, but there's another way to make leaf-shaped printers. Just trace the outline of a leaf onto heavy cardboard and cut it out. It won't dry out like a real leaf!

Gathering supplies

See what natural printers you can find when you are out on a walk. Some, such as feathers and bark, will keep for years, while green leaves will have to be used before they dry out.

Roll or brush thick paint carefully over the objects, and press them onto paper to make a print. Try different effects and colors. For example, a white leaf or fern print looks great on dark paper.

You can use feathers to create a birdbath picture like this.

14

Leaf prints

Leaves come in all shapes, sizes, and textures. Experiment with leaves from trees, flowers, and houseplants.

Brush paint onto the back of the leaf, where there is more texture.

WHAT YOU NEED:

- A collection of leaves—at least three different types
- Bright poster paint
- Paper • A brush

1 Brush a bright color on the back of a leaf, and press it down onto dark-colored paper. Make several prints, then let the paint dry.

2 Take a different leaf and a different color of paint. Print onto the paper, overlapping the first leaves if you wish.

3 Continue printing until hardly any of the dark background shows through.

Try printing while the first color is still wet. Use pale colors on white paper for an airy, delicate effect.

1

2

Mount your picture on colored paper, and hang it on your wall.

Potato prints

A potato printer is good for making bold prints. It's inexpensive, easy to make, and easy to use.

All you need to make a potato printer is a big potato and a craft knife. Your printer won't last very long, but if you slice off the old design, you can start again on the fresh surface. Other root vegetables make good printing blocks, too—try a few and see which ones work best.

WHAT YOU NEED:
- A large potato
- A sharp pencil
- A craft knife
- Thick paints
- Paper

1 Ask an adult to cut the potato in half. Draw a simple design on the cut surface with a sharp pencil. We made a butterfly, a flower, and a star.

2 Ask the adult to cut around the design and remove the excess from the edges so just your design sticks out. Brush paint over the surface of the design.

3 Press the painted surface firmly onto paper. Rock the printer gently, so that all parts of the design touch the paper.

Try colored paper and contrasting paints for gorgeous giftwrap.

TIP

It's fun to make your own gift tags. Cut lots of small rectangles from stiff colored paper and fold them in half. Punch a hole in one corner and tie a loop of ribbon or string on each tag. Then use potato printers to make a design on one side. Leave the other side blank so you have a place to write a message.

TIP

Use a small cookie cutter to make an instant printer! Just press the cutter into a freshly cut potato. Ask an adult to cut away the area around shape.

Your friends and family will love receiving a gift with a tag that's homemade by you!

TIP

Try using different colored paints on different parts of a printer to get some really interesting, multi-colored results!

Prints from food

It's amazing how many ready-to-use printers you can find right in your kitchen. Pasta comes in all kinds of unusual shapes, and fruit and vegetables can be cut into halves, circles, and quarters to make instantly printable designs.

Good enough to eat

Try using an orange slice, a cabbage leaf, half a bell pepper, or a carrot (cut into circles or sliced down the middle). Cut one apple lengthwise, and another crosswise, and compare the results. The possibilities for food printers are endless.

Foody wallpaper

Once you have experimented with different food prints, try making a wallpaper design. Draw light **guidelines** first with a ruler and pencil, and then build up a design using one, two, or three shapes.

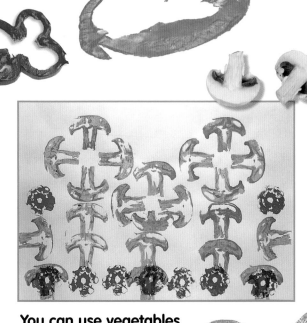

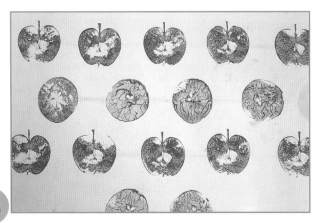

You can use vegetables and fruits to make eye-catching patterns or funky pictures like the flower garden shown above.

Market display

This is an impressive project you can make from materials you've got around the house. Make sure you ask an adult for permission before you raid the refrigerator for food printers!

WHAT YOU NEED:
- A cardboard box
- 2 cardboard tubes
- Fruits and vegetables
- Scissors
- A craft knife
- Poster paints
- Paper • Glue

1 Ask an adult to cut the side flaps off the box. The bottom flap will be the base, and the top flap supports the **awning**. Add **pillars** made from cardboard tubes. Glue these inside the outer edges of the box. Paint the inside of the box a light color.

2 Ask an adult to help cut the awning from cardboard. Paint it brightly. You could give your stand a name, too, and paint it on. Glue the awning to the front of the box and pillars.

3 Make lots of fruit and vegetable prints and cut them out. You'll need something to support them. Use smaller boxes or ask an adult to cut box shapes from white cardboard. Glue the boxes and prints to the front of the stall. The grapes can be hung from string.

Make an appetizing assortment of fruit and vegetable prints.

Make a Pop Art print

The artist **Andy Warhol** often repeated the same image several times to make bold, bright paintings and prints. Here's how to make a stunning Pop Art print, Warhol-style, for your wall.

WHAT YOU NEED:
- A ruler and a pencil
- Bright paints and a brush
- Bubble wrap (the kind with many small bubbles)
- Paper
- A black felt-tip pen
- A simple printer—this could be a cardboard or wooden block, a potato, or a piece of fruit
- Thick cardboard
- White glue

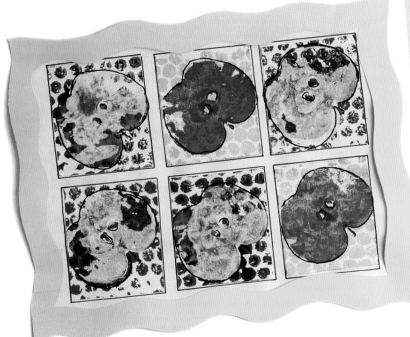

1 Brush brightly colored paint over the bubble wrap, and press it down onto the paper to print a dot pattern. Do this several times, and use a different color for each piece of paper. Use the ruler and pencil to cut the prints into neat squares, each the same size.

2 Arrange the squares in a **checkered** pattern and glue them to the cardboard. Leave a wide border. Brush paint over your printer and press it onto the first square. Choose a color that **contrasts** with the dots. **Complementary colors**—red and green, blue and orange, and yellow and purple—are great combinations.

3 Continue printing onto the squares until every one is filled. Use the black felt-tip to go over the border of each square. Cut some cardboard to make a frame. Paint it in a bright color and then cut a wavy outline with scissors. Tape a loop of yarn to the back so that you can hang it up.

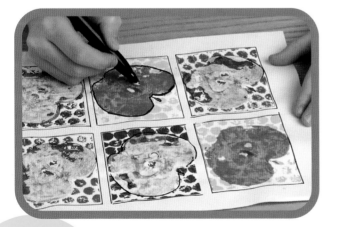

The dots in your picture will make it look like the prints that Andy Warhol made.

A Pop Art notebook cover

Make a design like the one above on a large sheet of paper (not cardboard). When the paint is dry, cover it with plastic wrap. Place an open notebook on the back of the print and trace around it. Draw a 2-inch border around the tracing. Cut slits at the corners of this border to make flaps. Fold the flaps over the edges of the book and glue them down. Then glue down the first and last pages of the book to cover the flaps.

Marbling

Marbling is a type of printing that uses oil paint and water to make patterns that are one-of-a-kind. The oil in the paint sits on the surface of the water, and makes it stick to the paper when you make a print.

Marbling paper

The paper for this project needs to be thick enough not to turn soggy in the water, but thin enough for you to be able to peel it off the surface.

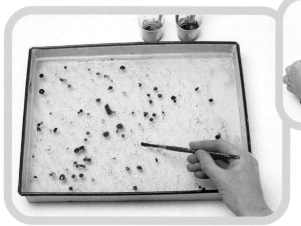

1 Mix oil paints with mineral spirits until they are runny enough to fall off the brush in blobs. Start with just two colors. Fill the pan halfway with water, then flick or pour the paint onto the surface. Swirl the surface gently with the end of a brush.

2 Lay a sheet of paper very gently on top of the water, smoothing away any air bubbles. Be careful not to push the paper under the surface.

3 Lift the paper gently from one end, and let it dry.

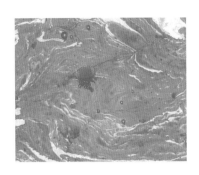

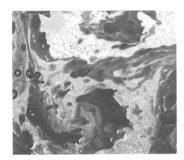

Marble collage

Marbled paper can be used to make great collages, with interesting patterns in the paint. Draw a simple picture on scrap paper. Cut up the picture, so that each object or area of the picture is a separate shape.

Trace these shapes onto different colors of marbled paper. Cut them out and fit them together like a puzzle. Glue the pieces of your marble collage to a new piece of paper.

TIP

Try adding a little wallpaper paste to the water—this makes a feathery pattern in the paint when you stir it. It's especially good for watery effects, such as in this pond.

23

Monoprints

A monoprint is made by pressing a piece of paper over a freshly painted design and lifting it off. The textures and shapes you get would be impossible to create by painting. Monoprints may not always be successful, but when they are, they can be fabulous!

TIP

When you roll your paint out onto the flat surface, try mixing two colors together to create an interesting shift between one color and the next. Experiment with multicolored monoprints, using lots of different colors.

You will need a really smooth surface to print from—an old countertop, a mirror, or a shiny baking sheet are ideal. Water-based printing inks give the best effects, but you can also use thick paint. Mix the paint with a little dishwashing detergent and white glue to keep it from drying out too quickly. As with the mirror prints on page 8, a monoprint (meaning "one print") can never be repeated.

CAUTION!

A sheet of glass is another surface you can use for making monoprints, but you will need an adult to help you. And be sure to get permission to paint on a counter, a table, or another piece of furniture.

Drawing a monoprint

In this project, you draw a shape to create a monoprint beneath.

WHAT YOU NEED:
- Thick paint or printing ink
- A smooth surface
- A roller or wide brush
- Paper

1 Roll or brush bands of color onto your smooth work surface, and place the paper lightly on top.

2 Using a pencil, crayon, or knitting needle, draw a design on the paper. Be careful to press down only where you are drawing.

3 Lift up the paper gently, making sure not smudge the image. Let it dry completely.

Stencils

Stenciling was very popular among the early pioneers, who couldn't buy wallpaper or decorated furniture. Practice stenciling on paper or cardboard first. Then, when you feel confident enough (and an adult says it's OK), you can use the stencils to decorate your bedroom.

Finding and using stencils

There are plenty of objects that are ready-made stencils. You can also buy stencils from craft stores, or make them yourself. To work with stencils, you will need a brush with short, stubby bristles. The paint should be almost dry, and you should dab it over the stencil. This technique is called stippling.

Make your own stencils

Stencils are a great way to show off your style. Decorate your notebooks, stationery, or even a t-shirt.

WHAT YOU NEED:
- Stiff stencil paper or thin cardboard
- A short-haired brush
- Thick paint • A pencil
- A craft knife
- Paper

1 Draw a simple design onto stencil paper or cardboard with a pencil.

2 Ask an adult to cut out the shape with a craft knife. This is your stencil.

3 Tape the stencil to a sheet of paper. Using a nearly dry brush, stipple the paint over the hole in the stencil, making sure that you paint right up to the edges.

Stencil spatter

Instead of stippling your stencil design, you can spatter! Just load the paint onto an old toothbrush, point the brush at the paper, and flick the bristles with your finger. Try using interesting shapes such as leaves, keys, or tools as a stencil. Spatter the items once, then move them slightly and spatter them again with another color.

TIP

Use a simple stenciled design to decorate writing paper and matching envelopes. Or stencil giftwrap— use spray paint for really quick results.

Spray stenciling

For really quick stenciling, you can use spray paint. Spray paints come in lots of interesting colors—we used silver.

1 Make a large stencil with a repeat pattern. Place it over colored paper and spray paint over it.

Instead of cutting holes, you can cut shapes, place them on the paper, and then spray them to get a negative image beneath.

2 Make sure you spray the entire stencil, then lift the stencil off. Let it dry for a few minutes. Repeat as needed to cover the paper.

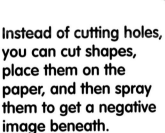

Printing pictures

The more you experiment with different kinds of printers, the more ideas you are likely to get for making pictures. You can mix prints with collage and paint effects, too. Try to think about your prints in a new way—a cabbage leaf print may look just like a cabbage leaf—but it would also make a great tree!

Trees in the park

In this project, you can use cabbage leaves to create fancy tree shapes that would take a long time to draw or paint.

WHAT YOU NEED:

- Cabbage leaves
- Thick paints
- Thin, watered-down paints
- Brushes • Paper
- Thick paper • Glue
- Scissors

A stippling brush (one with short, stiff bristles) is good for brushing paint onto the cabbage leaf.

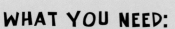

1 Paint the background very quickly, using a wide, soft brush and thin, watered-down paints. Let it dry. (Taping the paper to your work surface keeps the paper from wrinkling.)

2 On another piece of paper, make lots of tree prints using cabbage leaves of different sizes. Play with different **hues** ranging from yellow-green to forest green to brown.

3 When the trees are dry, cut them out and glue them to the picture. Finish the picture by printing a fence, using the edge of a piece of cardboard brushed with brown paint.

Can you make a print collage like this of your favorite place? Think about what printers you would use to make an ocean, a garden, or a city scene.

TIP

Cauliflower and broccoli make good trees, too. Simple shapes torn from paper make delicate clouds, misty mountains, icebergs, or rough rocks. Sandpaper is perfect for cliffs.

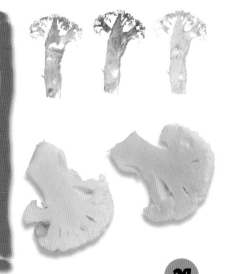

Glossary

Andy Warhol American artist famous for his colorful prints (1928–1987)

awning a sloped cover over a door or window that keeps the sun and rain off

checkered a pattern made up of squares of different colors

complementary colors colors that are opposite each other on the color wheel

construction paper thick, textured paper

contrast to stand out from things nearby because of visible differences. Colors contrast when they are very different from one another.

craft knife a thin pointed blade for making small, neat cuts. Ask an adult help you with this sharp tool.

guidelines lines on a piece of paper to help you place your images

hues different versions of the same color, such as lime green, kelly green, and forest green

mineral spirits a poisonous and dangerous liquid used to thin oil paints and clean oil paint from brushes

paint roller a rolling tool that spreads paint evenly over an area

pillars tall columns on a building

printers objects to which paint is applied to make a print

sketchbook a book for making quick drawings and designs

spattering to spray a picture by flicking paint off a brush

symmetrical a shape that is the same on both sides

Index

Notes for parents and teachers

The projects in this book can be used as stand-alone projects or as part of other areas of study. The ideas in the book offer children inspiration, but you should always encourage them to draw from their own imagination and first-hand observation.

Sourcing ideas

All art projects should tap into children's interests and be relevant to their lives and experiences. Some stimulating starting points include found objects, discussions about their family and pets, hobbies, TV shows, or current affairs.

Encourage children to source their own ideas and references, from books, magazines, or the Internet. Digital cameras are handy for recording reference materials (pictures of landscapes, people, or animals) that can be printed out to look at during a project.

Other lessons can be an ideal springboard for an art project—for example, a seasonal celebration such as Thanksgiving could be the start of a card-printing project, or a science lesson could lead to printing from seedheads or cross-sections of fruit.

Use recycling as a basis for print activities. Have children to come up with new uses for broken toys and other objects.

Encourage children to keep a sketchbook of their ideas, and to collect images and objects to help them develop their artwork.

Give children as many first-hand experiences as possible through visits and contact with creative people.

Evaluating work

It's important and motivating for children to share their work with others, and to compare ideas and methods. Encourage them to talk about their work. What do they like best about it? How would they do it differently next time?

Show the children examples of other artists' work. How did they tackle the same subject and problems? Do the children like the work? Why or why not?

Help children to recognize the originality and value of their work, to appreciate the different qualities in others' work, and to respect ways of working that are different from their own. Display children's work for all to admire!

Expanding the techniques

Look at ways to develop extensions to a project. For example, many of the ideas in this book could be adapted into painting, collage, and print-making. Use image-enhancing computer software and digital scanners to enhance, build up, and juxtapose images.

Help your artist(s) set up an art gallery to show off their work, or scan artwork and post the images to a photo website where others can log in and view them. Having their work displayed professionally will make them feel that their work is valued.